HORSE BREEDS

AMERICAN PAINT HORSES

by David Denniston

CAPSTONE PRESS
a capstone imprint

Snap Books are published by Capstone Press,
1710 Roe Crest Drive, North Mankato, Minnesota 56003
www.mycapstone.com

Library of Congress Cataloging-in-Publication Data
Library of Congress Cataloging-in-Publication Data is available
on the Library of Congress website.
ISBN: 978-1-5435-0033-2 (hardcover)
ISBN: 978-1-5435-0039-4 (paperback)
ISBN: 978-1-5435-0045-5 (eBook PDF)

Editorial Credits
Amy Kortuem, editor
Kayla Rossow, designer
Morgan Walters, media researcher
Kathy McColley, production specialist

Image Credits
Alamy: AF archive, 7, catnap, 15, 19, TOLBERT PHOTO, 25;
ASSOCIATED PRESS, 18; Dreamstime: Rancho, 9; Glow Images:
SuperStock, 5; Image Courtesy of the American Paint Horse Association,
23; iStockphoto: AStarphotographer, 29, DawnYL6161, 12, Zuzule, spread
16-17; Newscom: Marion Fichter imageBROKER, 11; Shutterstock:
CAESARstock, 24, Diane Garcia, 26, Irina Mos, spread 2-3, Juliata, (floral)
design element throughout, L. Kramer, (fish scale) design throughout,
Lenkadan, Cover, redstone, (paper background) design element
throughout, suns07butterfly, (watercolor) design element throughout,
Tootles, 20, yod67, (horse vector) design element, Zuzule, 1

Printed and bound in the USA.
010779S18

TABLE OF CONTENTS

Chapter 1
An American Horse 4

Chapter 2
A Horse of Many Colors. 10

Chapter 3
Western Pleasure Winners 18

Chapter 4
Paints in Action 24

Fast Facts 28
Glossary 30
Read More. 31
Internet Sites 31
Index. 32

CHapter 1
An American Horse

Hundreds of years ago early relatives of the American Paint Horse roamed the North American landscape. American Indians liked the horses for their color and calm personalities. Soon early U.S. settlers rode the spotted horses on ranches. The horses' eye-catching spots also made them popular in early U.S. Western shows.

Today Paints are a symbol of American history. Paints remind people of a time when the country's borders first began stretching from sea to sea.

American Indians have a long history of working with Paint horses.

Early Relatives of Paints

In 1519 explorer Hernán Cortés sailed from Spain to Mexico. Cortés wanted to find gold and claim land for Spain. Cortés brought 16 horses with him. One of these horses was brown with white spots.

Soon English, French, and other European explorers brought horses to North America. The spotted horse **mated** with these horses. Many of the spotted horse's offspring also had spots. These horses were early relatives of today's Paints.

Paints and American Indians

Some American Indians rode horses to help them hunt buffalo. They especially liked the spotted horses. The horses blended with the surroundings. This **camouflage** coloring helped Indians sneak up on buffalo. It also helped them hide from enemies during battles. Some American Indians believed the spotted horses had magical powers.

mate—to join together to produce young

camouflage—coloring that makes people, animals, or objects look like their surroundings

Paints as Movie Stars

American Paint horses are common stars in movies. They are especially popular in Western movies, where they are ridden by characters who play cowboys, ranchers, outlaws, sheriffs, and other roles.

Five Paint horses played the role of a legendary Spanish Mustang named Hidalgo in a 2004 movie of the same name. The horses had similar color patterns and appearances. They were chosen because they looked like Hidalgo, who was said to have won a 3,000-mile (4,828-kilometer) race across the Arabian desert. Some cast and crew members of the movie liked the Paints so much that they bought some of the horses to keep after filming was over.

PAINTS IN THE WEST

By the mid-1800s European settlers controlled much of the land where American Indians once lived. Many settlers in the western United States lived on large cattle ranches. The ranchers rode horses to help them herd cattle. They called spotted horses "Paints."

In the early 1900s the sport of rodeo became popular in the United States. Cowboys competed in several events related to ranching. Many rodeo riders impressed crowds on their fast, athletic Paints.

THE APHA

By the late 1950s Paint owners wanted to form a breed **registry** to keep track of each Paint's ancestry. In 1962 Rebecca Tyler Lockhart and other Paint owners started the American Paint Stock Horse Association. The name was later changed to the American Paint Horse Association (APHA).

Today more than 1 million horses are registered with the APHA. It is the second largest U.S. horse breed registry.

registry—an organization that keeps track of the ancestry for horses of a certain breed

Some people still use Paints on ranches.

Chapter 2

A Horse of Many Colors

The color patterns of Paints are their best-known feature. People often mate Paints with horses of other breeds and hope the foals will have the Paints' famous spots. But the Paint's color is only one of its admired features. Paints also are known for their calmness, strength, and speed.

COLORING

Many Paints have white spots on a dark coat color. Other Paints have dark spots on a white body. To be registered regularly by the APHA, a Paint must have at least one spot from the time of birth. The spot needs to be at least 2 inches (5 centimeters) wide and have unpigmented skin underneath. If the horse's body color is white, the spot must be of a contrasting color and pigmented skin must be underneath.

Horses in the regular registry must also have one other Paint horse trait, such as a mane that is white with another color. Solid-colored horses may be registered in the APHA's Solid Paint-bred registry.

The spots on each Paint have different patterns.

Tobiano Paints often have dark heads and white leg markings.

A Paint's coat can be almost any color. Black, bay, brown, buckskin, and chestnut are common. Bay horses are a shade of red-brown. They usually have black manes and tails. Buckskin Paints are tan, and chestnut horses are a copper color.

COAT PATTERNS

Paints have three main coat patterns. These patterns are the tobiano, overo, and tovero.

The tobiano pattern is the most common. The tobiano's spots often are rounded. White hair is common on all legs. Dark hair usually covers the flanks, or the fleshy area in front of the back legs. The tobiano's head often is dark.

The overo Paint usually has dark hair across its back. The overo's spots often appear scattered or splashy. Dark coloring is common on at least one leg.

The tovero is a mix of the overo and tobiano patterns. Many toveros have dark hair around the ears. Often, one or both eyes are blue.

MAIN FEATURES

The Paint is a stock horse. A stock horse has a large frame and a muscular body. To be registered each Paint must have parents that are registered as Paints, Quarter Horses, or Thoroughbreds.

The Paint's stock horse features are easy to recognize. It has a broad chest that leads to a finely muscled neck. The horse's strong legs and muscular hindquarters help it pick up speed quickly.

The height of a horse is measured from the ground to the **withers**. The height is measured in hands. A Paint usually is 14.2 to 16 hands tall. One hand equals 4 inches (10 cm).

FACT

Some Paint horses are born without spots. People sometimes call these horses breeding stock Paints. These Paints can produce foals with spots.

withers—the top of a horse's shoulders

PERSONALITY

Paints are calm. They often stay calm even in unfamiliar surroundings. Their personalities make them excellent horses for children.

Paints also are intelligent. People have success training Paints for almost any activity.

The Paint's calm personality makes it suitable for children.

muscular
hindquarters

strong legs

expressive eyes

finely muscled neck

broad chest

Chapter 3

Western Pleasure Winners

The Paint's athletic build allows it to perform well at competitions. Paint owners and their horses compete at thousands of horse shows each year.

HORSE SHOWS

Many horse shows are local or regional. Paints often compete against other breeds of horses at these shows. Some shows are recognized by the APHA. Only registered Paints can participate in these shows.

Many Paints compete in Western pleasure classes at shows.

Shows have several events called classes. Classes are offered for both youth and adults. People ride Paints in many classes. In halter classes competitors lead their horses. Horses are judged on their physical features in halter classes.

Keeping a steady pace is important in Western pleasure classes.

WESTERN PLEASURE

The Paint's eye-catching appearance and relaxed personality make it a tough competitor in the Western pleasure class. In this class riders ask their horses to perform three **gaits**. These gaits are the walk, the jog, and the lope.

Horses are judged according to their performance in the class. Each gait should be slow and smooth. Consistency is important in the Western pleasure class. Horses should keep their heads in about the same position throughout the class. Horses also should perform each gait at the same pace.

Horses must respond well to their riders in the Western pleasure class. They should quickly and calmly go from one gait to another.

gait—the manner in which a horse moves

Western Tack and Clothing

Competitors in the Western pleasure class use Western equipment, or tack. They use Western saddles. These large, sturdy saddles have a saddle horn. Some people use Western saddles that are decorated with silver in shows.

Western clothing is needed for the Western pleasure class. Competitors wear long-sleeved shirts, belts, cowboy hats, cowboy boots, and long pants. Many competitors wear chaps. These leather leggings fit over riders' pants.

Western Pleasure Training

Paints that are at least 2 years old usually are ready to be ridden. At first, trainers often attach a horse to a long rope called a longe line. The horse learns to respond to commands while moving in a circle around the trainer.

Soon, trainers fit a horse with a saddle and a **bridle**. A bridle includes straps that fit around a horse's head. It also has a metal **bit** that fits in the horse's mouth. Straps called reins lead from the bit to the rider.

bridle—the straps that fit around a horse's head and connect to a bit to control a horse while riding

bit—the metal mouthpiece of the bridle

People training horses for Western pleasure must ride often. They teach their horses to move slowly at each gait. The horses learn to bring their hind legs well underneath their bodies while moving. People also teach their horses to back up smoothly.

Yellow Mount – the "Face" of the APHA

A big overo stallion named Yellow Mount is probably the most recognized Paint horse in the world. His owners, Stanley and Jodie Williamson, had a famous artist do a painting of Yellow Mount with mares he had been bred with and the offspring. The APHA made reproductions of the painting and sent them around the world to promote the Paint breed. The APHA also used an image of Yellow Mount's head and face as part of its logo for many years.

Yellow Mount was the father of 26 APHA Champions and 11 National Champions. More than 100,000 Paint horses on APHA's registry are descendants of Yellow Mount. On April 1, 1990, the big stallion died at the age of 26.

CHAPTER 4

Paints in Action

The APHA holds the World Championship Show each September in Forth Worth, Texas. There are almost 300 classes with more than 1,000 registered Paints showing. The show gives out about $600,000 in cash and prizes.

The American Junior Paint Horse Association (AjPHA) Youth World Championship Show is for exhibitors ages 18 and younger. This annual summer show is the only all-scholarship championship horse show, and it gives out more than $130,000.

Paints often show their ranching skills at competitions.

Rodeos and Racing

Many Paints compete in events other than horse shows. Some Paints compete at rodeos. Rodeo events include calf roping and barrel racing. In calf roping riders chase a calf and use a rope to catch it. They then get off the horse and tie down the calf.

The exhibitor with the fastest time wins in barrel racing.

In barrel racing riders complete a pattern around three barrels. They try to do the pattern in the least amount of time without knocking down the barrels.

Paints' powerful hindquarters give them racing ability. The APHA has a racing program for registered Paints. Races take place in many states around the country.

FACT

Paint horses can run the distance of three football fields in less than 20 seconds.

OWNING A PAINT

Owning a Paint is rewarding, but it also is a big responsibility. Paints and other horses need a great deal of care. They need food, water, shelter, and exercise. Many people keep their Paints at their farms. Other owners pay to have their horses stay at another person's farm or stable.

Hundreds of years ago, a spotted horse from Europe led to the start of a new breed. Today the number of Paints in North America continues to soar. The colorful spotted horses will keep turning heads both in and out of the show ring.

Fast Facts:
The American Paint Horse

Name: During the 1800s and 1900s people had many names for early ancestors of Paints. People called them piebalds, skewbalds, and pintos.

History: In 1519 Spanish explorer Hernán Cortés brought a spotted horse to North America. The horse mated with other horses. The offspring of these horses were early relatives of today's Paints.

Height: Paints are 14.2 to 16 hands (about 5 feet or 1.5 meters) tall at the withers. Each hand equals 4 inches (10 centimeters).

Weight: 1,000 to 1,200 pounds (450 to 540 kilograms)

Colors: Most Paints have a solid body color and at least one white spot. Black, bay, brown, chestnut, and buckskin are common coat colors.

Features: muscular body frame; broad chest; flat forehead; small, pointed ears; strong legs; powerful hindquarters

Personality: calm, intelligent, cooperative

Abilities: Many people ride Paints in Western classes at horse shows. Paints also are good horses for rodeos, trail riding, and racing.

Life span: about 25 to 30 years

Glossary

bit (BIT)–the metal mouthpiece of the bridle

bridle (BRYE-duhl)–the straps that fit around a horse's head and connect to a bit to control a horse while riding

camouflage (KAM-uh-flahzh)–coloring that makes people, animals, or objects look like their surroundings

chaps (CHAPS)–leather leggings that fit over pants; chaps protect the legs of riders on horseback

gait (GATE)–the manner in which a horse moves; gaits include the walk, jog, and lope

longe line (LUNJ LINE)–a long rope that attaches to a horse; horses on a longe line are taught to move in a circle around the trainer while responding to verbal commands

mate (MAYT)–to join together to produce young

pigment (pig-MUHNT)–a substance that gives color to something

registry (REH-juh-stree)–an organization that keeps track of the ancestry for horses of a certain breed

withers (WITH-urs)–the top of a horse's shoulders

Read More

Graubart, Norman. *Horses in American History.* How Animals Shaped History. New York: PowerKids Press, 2015.

Kolpin, Molly. *Favorite Horses: Breeds Girls Love.* Crazy About Horses. North Mankato, Minn.: Capstone Press, 2015.

Osborne, Mary Pope, and Natalie Pope Boyce. *Horse Heroes.* Magic Tree House Fact Tracker. New York: Random House for Young Readers, 2013.

Internet Sites

Use FactHound to find Internet sites related to this book.

Visit *www.facthound.com*

Just type in 9781543500332 and go!

 Super-cool stuff! Check out projects, games and lots more at **www.capstonekids.com**

Index

American Indians, 4, 6, 8
American Junior Paint Horse Association
    (AjPHA), 24
American Paint Horse Association
    (APHA), 8, 10, 11, 18, 23, 24, 27

barrel racing, 26, 27

calf roping, 26
care, 27
chaps, 22
coat patterns, 12–13
    overo, 12, 13, 23
    tobiano, 13
    tovero, 12, 13
coloring, 10–11, 13
Cortés, Hernán, 6

gaits, 21, 23

Hidalgo, 7

Lockhart, Rebecca Tyler, 8

movies, 7

personality, 15

Quarter horses, 14

racing, 27
ranches, 4, 8
rodeos, 26

saddles, 22
size, 14
stock horses, 14

Thoroughbreds, 14

Western pleasure classes, 21–23
World Championship Show, 24

Yellow Mount, 23
Youth World Championship Show, 24